The Essence of America:
In Haiku

WALLACE G. BERGER

The Essence of America: In Haiku

Copyright © 2019 by Wallace G. Berger

All Rights Reserved.

ISBN: 9781691512676

Dedication

Dedicated to the United States of America, the country that provided me the opportunity to realize my dreams.

Acknowledgement

Charlene Berger, Jerry Gillmore, Ted Grocki, and Becky Zingarelli reviewed the manuscript and providing numerous suggestions that improved the quality and coverage of the poems. Had I followed all their recommendations the book might have been better. Thank you for exercising the values of generosity and truthfulness.

Wallace G. Berger

Introduction

These Haiku describe the essence of this wonderful country, a country that is an inspiration to, and aspiration of, countries all over the world. These poems encapsulate the enduring ideals that should guide our personal lives and our country's policies.

The 20 values that I consider essential to the American experience, and are referenced in the 300 Haiku are:
- Freedom to pursue happiness
- Religious freedom and freedom from religion
- Checks and balances and fair elections
- Justice under just laws
- Equality and civil rights
- Diversity/acceptance
- Civilian rule over the military
- Moral leadership
- Fairness
- Second chance
- Honesty/truthfulness
- Generosity
- Compassion/empathy
- Solidarity/community
- A better future
- Opportunity
- Achievement/education
- Curiosity and experimentation
- Sound environment
- Informality

Fear, tribalism, and personal gain can subvert the values that make America a moral leader. Wandering from our ideals may provide an illusion of protection, but we risk losing what we cherish. These poems remind us what is at stake.

At the back of this book I have included several blank pages for your notes. You may want to use these pages, to list other values that are central to your view of America and even write some Haiku to express what these values mean to you.

A Reader's Guide

These Haiku were developed following some of the traditional Japanese standards. In particular, you will note that, in most cases, the poems:

1. Have 3 lines consisting of 5/7/5 syllables per line
2. The first 5-syllable line in <u>combination</u> with the 7-syllable line is a phrase and the other 5-syllable line is a sentence fragment
3. Have no punctuation/capitalization, the reader provides these elements

Because the relationship of the phrase element of the poem to the fragment is often not obvious, a careful rereading of the poem may be rewarding. In most cases, the fragment introduces a new thought that is associated with the phrase – your challenge is to figure out how and which interpretation resonates with you.

To understand the structure of the poem you will have to add the punctuation. Reading the poem out loud is often the best way to discover where the pauses and inflections should be used.

A Reader's Guide

The format of placing no more than three poems on a page reinforces the need to take the time to focus on each poem before moving on.

Within the book, the poems are loosely organized by what I considered common themes – the 20 values. Because many of our Nation's values are closely related, some poems could have appeared in more than one place. For the purposes of this book, I placed the poems under the value that seemed to be the most relevant.

You may want to use the book as a companion during thoughtful periods by re-reading those Haiku (hence the poem numbers) that best support your introspection.

both phrase and fragment
combine to create image
others contemplate

Wallace G. Berger

Freedom to pursue happiness

freedom's constant lure
the license to be one's self
fulfill natures gift
[1]

yearning to breathe free
drawn to pursue freedom
those here those coming
[2]

**pursue happiness
freedom to talk and travel
ownership of self**
[3]

**live where you desire
work pray where ever you want
pursue all your dreams**
[4]

Wallace G. Berger

can't be selective
freedom is every ones right
exclusion makes slaves
[5]

**make your decisions
belief travel schools buying
rich world of options**
[6]

child leaves family
as foreigner leaves country
have independence
[7]

**laws protect others
life property civil rights
otherwise we free**
[8]

**happiness our role
government set the table
shelter food and health**
[9]

value each other
happiness comes easier
welfare of nation
[10]

**our experience
teaches to perfect values
change better than good**
[11]

**following your will
doing no harm to other
staying in your lane**
[12]

**set personal goals
within legal moral bounds
in line with values**
[13]

**fearful or fulfilled
contrast between slave and free
the land of the free**
[14]

**putting life at risk
for an abstract ideal
freedom's gravity**
[15]

Religious freedom and freedom from religion

**religious freedom
and freedom from religion
inner commitment**
[16]

**believe what you want
honor my beliefs as well
no coercion here**
[17]

what is religion
free to think and assemble
subset of freedom
[18]

religion is choice
belief guides your adherence
not inborn dictate
[19]

attendance option
worship in none one many
follow your own path
[20]

**proselytizing
not a national value
religion by choice**
[21]

Wallace G. Berger

**religious teachings
should not conflict with values
slowly evolving**
[22]

some require desire
religious beliefs inspire
for all to respect
[23]

not how you worship
living caring moral life
the mark of good soul
[24]

religious contrast
is less than what we all share
moral conduct code
[25]

**a secular group
can have our nation's values
what not how believe**
[26]

god knows the righteous
judge not so you be not judged
understand welcome
[27]

gods are merciful
forgiving promotes good deeds
values are valued
[28]

**religions exist
every god is good for some
each free to believe**
[29]

Wallace G. Berger

**religious morals
constitution and values
requires vigilance**
[30]

Wallace G. Berger

Checks and balances/fair elections

many checks balances
no supreme authority
kings not welcome here
[31]

protecting ourselves
no dictators crooks tyrants
wise founding fathers
[32]

**checking corruption
constitution loyalty
constructive tension**
[33]

each branch has bias
sum results in the balance
each has a clear role
[34]

**disenfranchising
leaves us all in jeopardy
every person counts**
[35]

**representation
no group discrimination
not american**
[36]

**loving the country
take part maintaining values
enfranchising all**
[37]

**representation
backbone of democracy
people must govern**
[38]

**members of congress
people's representatives
work for all of us**
[39]

**elected by all
government represents all
no lesser people**
[40]

make it hard to vote
targeting minorities
unamerican
[41]

full fair elections
all are encouraged to vote
everyone owns it
[42]

one side not enough
consensus for big issues
ruling near middle
[43]

compromise approach
evolutionary acts
no erratic swings
[44]

**from and to people
the government is a gift
safe free and happy**
[45]

Wallace G. Berger

Justice under just laws

**nation under law
peers dispense equal justice
empathy tempered**
[46]

**justice wears blindfold
doesn't matter who you are
based on what you did**
[47]

**same or different
race religion or beliefs
unbiased justice**
[48]

**truth and justice too
both independent of wealth
so goes theory**
[49]

Wallace G. Berger

**just and fair verdict
matching conditions offense
representative**
[50]

**can't be rule of law
with biased application
unsustainable**
[51]

Wallace G. Berger

jury of your peers
understanding dynamics
culture is factor
[52]

legitimacy
laws that don't discriminate
fairness is binding
[53]

appropriate fair
managed with equality
laws we can live with
[54]

**bipartisan laws
majority of people
confidence that fair**
[55]

**laws are quickly changed
when shown to discriminate
unintended woes**
[56]

**always innocent
until proven otherwise
not propaganda**
[57]

key legal focus
protect individual
build community
[58]

to protect people
not for extracting revenge
rehab is end game
[59]

all equal treatment
arrest conviction sentence
one humanity
[60]

Wallace G. Berger

Equality and civil rights

47

basic civil rights
public places homes jobs vote
what you are not who
[61]

our rights civil rights
all part of society
protecting us all
[62]

**no persecution
origin beliefs speaking
free to contribute**
[63]

**common needs desires
common heritage and genes
common way treated**
[64]

**not birth accident
character rather than fate
measures each person**
[65]

**increase female role
moderating contention
building the middle**
[66]

**whether black brown red
yellow or white all people
different not worse**
[67]

not money or tribe
character defines person
behavior is key
[68]

do unto others
giving others what you want
another human
[69]

every voter counts
engaging electorate
collective wisdom
[70]

55

in home of the free
all must enjoy civil rights
all or none at all
[71]

more education
equality catalyst
values morals too
[72]

fair and just taxes
equitable services
equal protection
[73]

resources to pay
services based on your need
human safety net
[74]

forgiveness trumps hate
compassion over disdain
embrace not deride
[75]

Diversity/acceptance

why did they come here
make better family life
it's america
[76]

**provide a haven
for the world's persecuted
religious foundation**
[77]

**escape certain death
immigration saving lives
grateful citizens**
[78]

work for better life
occupy the job ladder
tax and job engine
[79]

immigration gift
new ideas new sources
expanded gene pool
[80]

**immigrants impact
adrenaline infusion
our economy**
[81]

**first generation
millions of jobs created
they thank us we them**
[82]

**enriching gene pool
diversity of background
bring abilities**
[83]

**to be world leader
requires world understanding
using the best minds**
[84]

**over 500,000 veterans
loyal foreign immigrants
this is their proud home**
[85]

**fear of different
don't look talk and eat like me
humans all the same**
[86]

**hang with comfort folks
stretch your associations
learn from all people**
[87]

**no diversity
very boring existence
expanded options**
[88]

**treated with respect
to maintain their dignity
what we all expect**
[89]

at some point in time
ancestors were accepted
our turn to welcome
[90]

Wallace G. Berger

Civilian rule over the military

**citizens' army
civilian control enshrined
constitutional**
[91]

**civil decisions
over the military
people have power**
[92]

**civilian power
protecting democracy
dictators disdain**
[93]

**civilian control
guided by code of conduct
loyal to values**
[94]

**people safe without
use of war's battle weapons
second amendment**
[95]

**safeguarding country
represent all the people
serving with respect**
[96]

**protecting freedom
respect for people who serve
redress oppression**
[97]

**patriotism means
homage to constitution
rule of law prevails**
[98]

training in values
syncing up with civilians
different clothing
[99]

Wallace G. Berger

**military's oath
check presidential power
performing both ways**
[100]

follow those who care
respect with admiration
utmost effective
[101]

Wallace G. Berger

**values role model
chief responsibility
moral example**
[102]

foreign aggression
not empowered to police
by and for people
[103]

at home and abroad
governed by code of conduct
projecting values
[104]

**our military
like congress executive
serving the people**
[105]

Wallace G. Berger

Moral leadership

**our strength in the world
based on moral leadership
recognized virtue**
[106]

**leading from values
promoting free happy life
at home and abroad**
[107]

**among world nations
striving to be most admired
life full of promise**
[108]

**sharing with the world
our values and our virtues
a shining city**
[109]

**make others believe
consistent talk and action
a trusted leader**
[110]

**emerging nations
democratic guidance help
world community**
[111]

**world needs a model
democracy decency
reliable goals**
[112]

**supporting the right
beyond expediency
steadfast adherence**
[113]

**look at our values
like studying the bible
using today's lens**
[114]

**pervasive impact
religion basis of laws
our moral compass**
[115]

**kinder peaceful world
democracy shuns conflicts
our role is valued**
[116]

**freedom is the goal
peace and wellbeing its prize
making us secure**
[117]

**being a model
actions driven by values
a righteous person**
[118]

**actions match values
a trusted leadership role
a world role model**
[119]

**enduring values
thinking of what to pass on
a meaningful life**
[120]

Fairness

what do we expect
equal unbiased proper
all takes on fairness
[121]

people government
are committed to fairness
being trustworthy
[122]

93

be treated fairly
the oldest of emotions
reaffirming self
[123]

everyone succeeds
in pursuit of happiness
social safety net
[124]

95

honest effort pay
admiration for hard work
financial bonus
[125]

**fair for family
is what is fair for others
it spreads like blessing**
[126]

**get what you deserve
person and contributor
all merit fairness**
[127]

**pay justice treatment
same result for same action
human dignity**
[128]

**making your own way
being judged on your merits
fair recognition**
[129]

**even with good luck
we need predictable world
no moving goalposts**
[130]

taking the right change
returning the lost wallet
a truthful witness
[131]

**who says don't be fair
apply equally to us
view of hypocrites**
[132]

**when is it unfair
what would we like to happen
let's remedy it**
[133]

**without being fair
the strong evil dominate
society fails**
[134]

**fairness has big role
support of other values
foundation principle**
[135]

Second chance

**who needs second chance
who has not made a mistake
who am i to judge**
[136]

**big mistakes are made
we forgive if not forget
repentance is core**
[137]

**within religion
redo is fundamental
moral roots are deep**
[138]

**constantly evolve
learning changing from mistakes
redemption rebirth**
[139]

**rethinking our lives
major reflection milestone
self redirection**
[140]

**jail time for rehab
new attitudes behavior
welcome back my friend**
[141]

**punish or rehab
cost benefit decision
not even close call**
[142]

**no second chances
to capital punishment
justice not perfect**
[143]

**training counseling
forgiveness and compassion
our duty to help**
[144]

Wallace G. Berger

start over is hard
local national support
you are not alone
[145]

try to make it right
granting a fresh start to all
goodwill recycling
[146]

**chance to contribute
a life too precious to waste
it helps everyone**
[147]

**give a chance take one
a gift to change a lifetime
chance is not by chance**
[148]

**when you have nothing
no home no job no transport
second chance sole chance**
[149]

**we learn from mistakes
not branded for entire life
who could oppose it**
[150]

Honesty/truthfulness

**good to walk the talk
when words and deeds don't sync up
what can you count on**
[151]

honesty builds trust
relationships built on trust
required for bonding
[152]

**tell it to me straight
to be able to believe
look me in the eye**
[153]

**handshake is your bond
business personal foundation
liars not trusted**
[154]

**i can count on you
we teach it early to kids
even when it's tough**
[155]

you can bet your life
words are basis of action
create certainty
[156]

**progress needs teamwork
leadership is built on trust
honesty builds trust**
[157]

**honesty valued
telling truth and acting too
trust builds relations**
[158]

**on understanding
reputations made or lost
bet on honesty**
[159]

**when once dishonest
tough to mend reputation
best to keep it real**
[160]

earning your own way
don't take advantage of weak
yours belongs to you
[161]

**patience empathy
need to know the whole story
nothing omitted**
[162]

**tempered with prudence
honest without offending
feelings do matter**
[163]

**justice seeks the truth
honesty is an ally
for wise decisions**
[164]

in those who matter
need belief and confidence
counting on others
[165]

Generosity

**for our common good
we provide hand when needed
strengthen our country**
[166]

**how can i help you
building a stronger country
making all better**
[167]

**helping a neighbor
what goes around comes around
we are family**
[168]

Wallace G. Berger

good samaritan
helping even the stranger
out of many one
[169]

build bonds of kindness
feeling included wanted
values taught at home
[170]

learn this as parents
then teach it to your children
practice in village
[171]

family and friends
the needy and to cheer up
giving and sharing
[172]

sharing your blessings
give others time things money
building your karma
[173]

even caring words
easier give than accept
reflect on blessings
[174]

**values complement
generous compassionate
morality linked**
[175]

without being asked
without the recognition
act is the reward
[176]

gift of loving care
feeling appreciated
person of value
[177]

receiving a gift
feeling of obligation
pass on the favor
[178]

**giving affects lots
the way you and others feel
empowered to help**
[179]

**learn from each other
offer without being asked
reward in giving**
[180]

Wallace G. Berger

Compassion/empathy

spirit embraccs
all on this little blue ball
human compassion
[181]

**the less fortunate
our responsibility
moral commandment**
[182]

**pleasure in helping
each favor done adds karma
being good person**
[183]

**helping is in us
lending a tool or a hand
a good connection**
[184]

lifting others up
especially the weakest
sharing love with all
[185]

143

even with strangers
much easier to be kind
paying it forward
[186]

**compassion fills soul
growing and guiding our life
forgiveness frees us**
[187]

**love for all children
empathy for wellbeing
care across borders**
[188]

**care about the young
vulnerable among us
DNA and social too**
[189]

**imagine your kids
compared to disadvantaged
could be the reverse**
[190]

**some down but not out
opportunity for all
easily be me**
[191]

**people remember
the downtrodden the neglected
for the grace of god**
[192]

**tugging on your heart
seeing hearing suffering
feeling their aching**
[193]

**even the youngest
feels for others suffering
a survival gene**
[194]

wanting for others
blessings you have and they should
human compassion
[195]

Wallace G. Berger

Solidarity/community

**being supportive
stand up with nation allies
for common values**
[196]

fighting for country
family and our values
the united states
[197]

fight for our freedoms
willingness to sacrifice
country provides rights
[198]

**work on consensus
containing extremes movements
nurturing respect**
[199]

**welcoming feeling
our fellow americans
common values goals**
[200]

encourage neighbors
uphold the country's values
sharing a conscience
[201]

those sharing the town
parts of social mosaic
each piece makes the whole
[202]

**your community
an extended family
look after children**
[203]

**individuals
make made by community
interdependence**
[204]

Wallace G. Berger

**religious morals
proscribed values behavior
consensus baseline**
[205]

try to please others
people want to do right thing
like herd animals
[206]

**form of tribalism
it includes entire country
we are unified**
[207]

**elders' sacred trust
children's model for values
pledge to our nation**
[208]

Wallace G. Berger

161

**form personal bonds
improving social setting
extended kinfolk**
[209]

values in common
the whole stronger than its parts
each a testament
[210]

A better future

**america's lure
for better life each and all
the promise still lives**
[211]

all parents share dream
raise their kids with love and hope
dream is for success
[212]

pass on lineage
populating the future
better life for kids
[213]

giving life meaning
building your children's future
flourishing gene pool
[214]

better for our kids
improvement for our parents
for society
[215]

critical belief
living standards get better
promise is progress
[216]

**restless to advance
nation of working people
all ingredients**
[217]

**preoccupation
working planning every day
realizing dream**
[218]

**business government
setting table for future
people make effort**
[219]

kids starving mourning
afraid tired cold and alone
innocents suffer
[220]

grief encompasses
all those touched by injustice
humanity cries
[221]

**faith luck and hard work
count on life getting better
cornerstone of dream**
[222]

**new american
each generation prepares
assimilation**
[223]

**learn language customs
acquire education clothes
moving with the crowd**
[224]

**motivating growth
our belief in better life
present to future**
[225]

Opportunity

**opportunity
makes dream possible for all
we all qualify**
[226]

**part of our nature
seek out opportunities
elevate status**
[227]

**constant advancement
each generation better
education key**
[228]

**taking advantage
education prepares us
grasping the moment**
[229]

chance and networking
try to capitalize on
regional support
[230]

role for government
preparing for the future
policies and funds
[231]

prepared for success
needed skills equal access
governmental role
[232]

not DNA it's culture
teaching the young to fit in
burden is on us
[233]

**analyzing trends
finding opportunity
proactive approach**
[234]

**all who qualify
can seek opportunity
get best of the best**
[235]

**the best employee
no bias for job offer
enterprise success**
[236]

**for all the people
wellbeing builds strong nation
middle class engine**
[237]

**same thing forever
improvement requires some change
accept discomfort**
[238]

having lucky break
bringing your friends along too
joy deeper when shared
[239]

a hand up not out
honest work for honest pay
life meaning through work
[240]

Achievement/education

being productive
being a problem solver
being a hero
[241]

position in life
our economic status
one self worth measure
[242]

**still silver bullet
it is a door opener
education first**
[243]

**educated mind
learning promotes sound thinking
achievement fact based**
[244]

**free education
investment in our future
building a nation**
[245]

**our free public schools
becoming good citizens
accepting others**
[246]

chance for advancement
education work way up
making investment
[247]

Wallace G. Berger

**parents share wisdom
children gain apply knowledge
families advance**
[248]

**child's accomplishments
recognition of parents
apple falls near tree**
[249]

**to make life better
innovate create explore
catalysts for change**
[250]

**solving human woes
relying on science wealth
for the common good**
[251]

Wallace G. Berger

**tangible results
product to evaluate
concrete not concept**
[252]

**finding tomorrow
anticipate required skills
work stays relevant**
[253]

**life government law
tradition and commitment
slowly improving**
[254]

**pursuing a dream
follow opportunity
betting on yourself**
[255]

Wallace G. Berger

Curiosity and experimentation

**like to solve problems
find better ways to do things
a curious breed**
[256]

what makes things happen
how can i make world better
make a difference
[257]

an inventive lot
process to technology
motives to think big
[258]

want to mold our world
make life easier richer
sync up with values
[259]

**find problem to fix
innovate a solution
focus and effort**
[260]

.

**improving your life
the easiest best cheapest
find innovations**
[261]

**keep solving problems
improvement motivates us
engaged rewarded**
[262]

**solving big problems
is lucrative endeavor
analysis pays**
[263]

accept and seek change
progress has consequences
some unintended
[264]

rely on science
find the facts solve the problem
belief not enough
[265]

some of the brightest
use scientific method
searching for the truth
[266]

determining facts
peer review validated
consensus driven
[267]

understand nature
an interest in the real
knowing how world works
[268]

slowly perfecting
more perfect society
experimenting
[269]

challenge to improve
we readily embrace change
create wealth and time
[270]

Wallace G. Berger

Sound environment

**sacrcd covenant
stewardship of the planet
offspring legacy**
[271]

**treating the planet
as future's custodian
protecting unborn**
[272]

**good custodians
creatures earth air and water
can't restore extinct**
[273]

**studying nature
making it match to our needs
stewardship fine line**
[274]

**preserve heritage
great pressure to pillage land
many ways say no**
[275]

**health and happiness
connectivity with earth
nature's heritage**
[276]

Wallace G. Berger

**see environment
self image deeply hidden
memories prevail**
[277]

immersed in nature
engaging all the senses
diverting the mind
[278]

walking in mountains
nature is spiritual
beauty draws us in
[279]

inspiring surrounds
what are we without nature
part of living web
[280]

Wallace G. Berger

reverence for world
invokes respect for others
every thing living
[281]

every clement
natural environment
benefits others
[282]

**human's home planet
claim responsibility
management and care**
[283]

**license to despoil
legacy for our children
optimize what when**
[284]

211

**it belongs to all
balance one versus us all
a permanent trust**
[285]

Informality

**it's not who you are
respected for what you do
deeds not lineage**
[286]

**all regular folks
equal status and treatment
no entitlement**
[287]

**informality
provides opportunity
pals collaborate**
[288]

**respect for actions
country without royalty
praise for being good**
[289]

**not in this country
reaction to royalty
shun a class system**
[290]

216

**all americans
under one constitution
no untouchables**
[291]

**not too proud to help
those of different status
easily be me**
[292]

**the most powerful
relating to the weakest
able to listen**
[293]

**making decisions
authority not enough
truth must be ally**
[294]

**decision basis
subject to challenge on facts
facts democratic**
[295]

**you can buy comfort
not favoritism with law
universal rights**
[296]

**be approachable
at work home play and with friends
open and humble**
[297]

**as approachable
admit errors offenses
respect respected**
[298]

**you can always learn
backgrounds experiences
something from others**
[299]

**human dignity
nation of the common man
equality all**
[300]

Wallace G. Berger

My notes and poems
(Page 1)

My notes and poems
(Page 2)

Wallace G. Berger

My notes and poems
(Page 3)

My notes and poems
(Page 4)

Wallace G. Berger

My notes and poems
(Page 5)

My notes and poems
(Page 6)

Wallace G. Berger

My notes and poems
(Page 7)

My notes and poems
(Page 8)

My notes and poems
(Page 9)

My notes and poems
(Page 10)

About the author

Dr. Wallace G. Berger's background includes work as a researcher, scientist, U.S. Senate Staffer, system engineer, and program evaluator. He is the co-founder of a consulting company and is an active wood artist. His published books address contemporary social issues including climate change, the environment, loving relationships, aging, drug addition, grief, and gun violence.